COOKING
IN THE KITCHEN WITH
S·A·N·T·A

ILLUSTRATED BY TERESA B. RAGLAND

Ideals Children's Books • Nashville, Tennessee

TABLE OF CONTENTS

Copyright © 1992 by Ideals Publishing Corporation
All rights reserved.
Printed and bound in the United States of America
Published by Ideals Publishing Corporation
Nashville, Tennessee 37214
ISBN 0-8249-3096-7
Edited by Heidi King.
Designed by Margot Wind.

TABLE OF EQUIVALENTS

	U.S. Standard	Metric		U.S. Standard	Metric
Butter/margarine	1 tablespoon	15 grams	Sugar, brown	1 tablespoon	10 grams
	1/2 cup	125 grams		1/2 cup	80 grams
Flour, sifted, all-purpose	1/2 cup	60 grams		1 cup	160 grams
	1 cup	128 grams	Other ingredients	1 dry ounce	28 grams
Fruit, dried	2 cups	500 grams		1 pound	373 grams
Gelatin, granulated	1 cup	150 grams		1 liquid ounce	29.5 milliliters
Salt	1 teaspoon	5 grams		1 cup	.24 liter
Spices, ground	1 teaspoon	2 1/2 grams		1 pint	.47 liter
	2 tablespoons	15 grams		1 quart	.95 liter
Sugar, granulated	1 teaspoon	5 grams		1 gallon	3.8 liters
	1 tablespoon	15 grams	Oven temperatures	230°F	110°C
	1/4 cup	60 grams		275°F	135°C
	1 cup	240 grams		325°F	163°C
Sugar, confectioners'	1/4 cup	35 grams		350°F	176°C
	1/2 cup	70 grams		375°F	190°C
	1 cup	140 grams		400°F	204°C

To convert inches to centimeters, multiply by 2.54. For example: 13" x 2.54 = 33 cm.

BEFORE YOU START

Always get permission before beginning to cook and make sure an adult is nearby in case assistance is needed.

Read the recipe before starting, and make sure that all of the ingredients and equipment are on hand.

Wear an apron, wash hands thoroughly, and tie back long hair.

Gather the equipment and ingredients listed in the recipe.

Measure the ingredients listed in the recipe.

Ask an adult to help when cutting or chopping. Always cut in a downward motion, with the knife blade toward the cutting board, and keep fingers out of the way.

Keep the work area tidy. Put food away as soon as possible, especially items needing refrigeration. Clean up spills immediately to prevent accidents.

Don't forget to clean up after you cook. Put everything away and leave a clean kitchen.

3

COOKING SAFETY

Before using a sharp knife, can opener, broiler, blender, mixer, microwave, range, or oven, be sure an adult is present to help you.

Ask an adult to drain large amounts of food which have been cooked in hot water. If done incorrectly, the steam from the water can cause burns.

Turn the pan handles so that they do not hang over the edge of the range or over another burner.

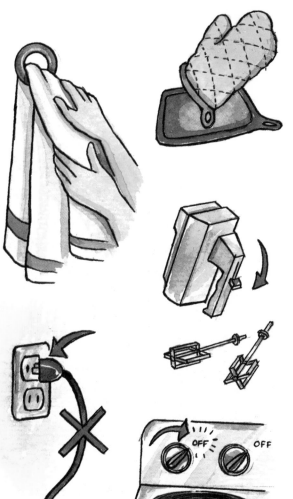

Use thick, dry pot holders—if they are thin or wet, pot holders will not provide adequate protection from the heat.

Be sure to dry your hands after washing to avoid electrical shock.

Turn off blender or mixer before scraping the sides of a container so that rubber spatula or spoon does not get caught in blades.

Turn off and unplug mixer before putting beaters into or taking them out of mixer.

Never disconnect an appliance by pulling on the cord; turn it off first, then pull the plug itself out of the socket.

Be sure to turn off the oven or range when finished cooking.

USING APPLIANCES

THE CONVENTIONAL OVEN

Move oven shelves to the correct position before turning the oven on.

Preheat oven as directed in each recipe.

Allow plenty of air space around each item baking—containers should not touch each other.

Alternate positioning of foods on each shelf so that one is not directly over another.

Use a tight-fitting cover or aluminum foil when a recipe calls for covering the pan.

Close the oven door quickly so that heat will not escape.

Place baking pans or sheets in center of oven when possible.

THE RANGE

Place large pans on large burners and small pans on small burners.

Turn the pan handles so they do not hang over the edge of the range or over another burner.

THE MICROWAVE OVEN

Read your microwave oven instruction booklet to find out which foods your oven can cook.

Cover foods as instructed to prevent spattering. Do not use foil.

Allow foods to stand for a few minutes after removal from the oven, because they continue to cook.

Be careful to avoid burns. Microwaves go through containers without heating them, but the food in the container often heats the container—they are often *very* hot.

COOKING AND BAKING TERMS

BATTER: A thin mixture of flour and liquid which is combined with other ingredients to make foods such as cakes.

BEAT: To make ingredients smooth with a brisk spoon motion or through the use of an electric mixer.

BLEND: To combine thoroughly two or more ingredients.

BOIL: To raise the temperature of water or another liquid until bubbles are breaking the surface. The boiling temperature of water is 212° F or 100° C.

COMBINE: To stir together two or more ingredients.

CREAM: To make a mixture smooth, light, and fluffy by beating with a spoon or electric mixer.

DOUGH: A thick mixture of flour and liquid which is combined with other ingredients to make recipes such as cookies.

FOLD: To gently combine two mixtures by moving a rubber spatula through the mixtures in a sliding and cutting motion.

KNEAD: To work into a uniform mixture by pressing, folding, and stretching.

STIR: To mix ingredients with a spoon in a circular motion.

WHIP: To beat rapidly to increase the volume of an ingredient such as heavy cream or egg whites.

MEASURING EQUIPMENT AND METHODS

Dry measure cups are for measuring dry ingredients such as flour, sugar, cornstarch, and other dry ingredients. For most dry ingredients, just fill the measuring cup and then level it with a spatula or kitchen knife. Brown sugar is measured differently—it is packed firmly and then leveled off. Shortening and peanut butter are also measured in a dry measuring cup because they must be packed before leveling off.

Glass measures are used for measuring liquids. They have spouts for pouring liquids without spilling. To measure accurately, bend down so your eyes are level with the measurement mark you need. Slowly pour in the liquid; stop when it reaches the correct mark.

Measuring spoons are used for measuring small amounts, either dry or liquid. Fill the spoon with the ingredient, and if dry, level with a spatula or kitchen knife. Brown sugar and shortening must be packed in spoons before leveling.

Butter and margarine are very easy to measure: 1 stick is equal to 1/2 cup. Their wrappers are often marked in tablespoons. Just cut through the wrapper and stick at the correct measurement line.

Never measure directly over mixing bowl because spillovers will affect your recipes.

MEASURING EQUIVALENTS

3 teaspoons = 1 tablespoon

1/2 tablespoon = 1 1/2 teaspoons

4 tablespoons = 1/4 cup

5 tablespoons + 1 teaspoon = 1/3 cup

2 cups = 1 pint

4 cups = 2 pints = 1 quart

4 quarts = 1 gallon

BUTTER OR MARGARINE MEASURING EQUIVALENTS

1/2 stick = 1/8 pound = 1/4 cup

1 stick = 1/4 pound = 1/2 cup

4 sticks = 1 pound = 2 cups

BEVERAGES

Sleigh Ride . . . . Makes 4 servings

INGREDIENTS:

12 ice cubes
1/2 cup chilled cranberry juice
1/2 cup chilled pineapple juice
1/2 cup chilled apple juice
1/2 cup chilled ginger ale
 2 tablespoons chilled grenadine, optional
    Bottle of chilled sparkling grape juice
1/2 lime

EQUIPMENT:

Measuring cups and spoons
Large jar with screwtop lid
4 glasses
Knife

1. Combine ice cubes, cranberry, pineapple, and apple juices, ginger ale,
   and grenadine, if desired, in a large jar with screwtop lid; shake well.
2. Remove ice cubes; place 2 or 3 in each glass. Discard remaining ice cubes.
3. Pour equal amounts of mixture into each glass.
4. Fill remainder of each glass with grape juice.
5. Cut lime into round slices with knife. Cut 2 round slices in half.
6. Garnish each glass with a lime slice
   and serve immediately.

Christmas Red Punch . . . . Makes 16 to 20 servings

INGREDIENTS:

1 pint strawberries
1/2 gallon vanilla ice cream, softened
1 liter strawberry soda
1 liter ginger ale

EQUIPMENT:

Knife
Punch bowl
Mixing spoon
Ladle
Punch cups

1. Combine ice cream, strawberry soda, and ginger ale in a punch bowl.
   Stir with mixing spoon to blend.
2. Gently pull hulls from strawberries or hull with knife.
3. Add strawberries to punch and stir with mixing spoon.
4. Let stand for 1 hour. Stir punch with mixing spoon.
5. Ladle equal amounts of punch into each punch cup and serve.

Sparkling Holiday Punch . . . . Makes 9 servings

INGREDIENTS:

2/3 cup sugar
2/3 cup water
  1 cup grapefruit juice
1/2 cup orange juice
  3 tablespoons grenadine, optional
  1 liter chilled ginger ale

EQUIPMENT:

Measuring cups and spoons
Large saucepan
Mixing spoon
Punch bowl
Ladle
Punch cups

1. Combine sugar and water in saucepan; stir over MEDIUM heat with mixing spoon until sugar is dissolved. Boil 10 minutes; cool.
2. Add juices to sugar mixture; chill in refrigerator thoroughly.
3. Pour juices, ginger ale, and grenadine, if desired, into punch bowl.
4. Ladle equal amounts into each punch cup and serve.

Hot Spiced Cider . . . . Makes 6 to 8 servings

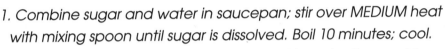

INGREDIENTS:

  1 quart apple cider
  8 whole cloves
  1 large cinnamon stick
1/8 teaspoon nutmeg
  3 tablespoons fresh lemon juice
  1 lemon, optional
    Whole cloves for garnish, optional

EQUIPMENT:

Measuring cups and spoons
Large saucepan
Knife
Strainer
Ladle
Mugs

1. Combine cider, cloves, cinnamon stick, nutmeg, and lemon juice in saucepan over MEDIUM-LOW heat; cover and heat 30 minutes.
2. Cut lemon into 6 slices with knife; stud each with whole cloves, if desired.
3. Strain cider, discard cinnamon stick and cloves. Ladle equal amounts into mugs.
4. Garnish each mug with clove-studded lemon slices, if desired, and serve.

Spicy Chocolate Eggnog . . . . **Makes 6 servings**

INGREDIENTS:

- 4 eggs
- 2 cups milk
- 1 cup heavy whipping cream
- 1/2 cup chocolate syrup
- 1/2 cup unsifted confectioners' sugar
- 1/8 teaspoon cinnamon
- 1/8 teaspoon nutmeg

EQUIPMENT:

Measuring cups and spoons
Electric blender
Punch cups

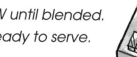

1. Combine all ingredients in blender container.
2. Cover and blend mixture on LOW until blended.
3. Cover and chill eggnog until ready to serve.

Christmas Wassail . . . . **Makes 24 servings**

INGREDIENTS:

- 1 gallon apple juice
- 1 quart orange juice
- 2 cups fresh lemon juice
- 1 cup plus 2 tablespoons sugar
- 1 can (16 ounces)
  frozen pineapple juice, thawed
- 2 cinnamon sticks
- 2 teaspoons whole cloves

EQUIPMENT:

Measuring cups and spoons
Large kettle
Strainer
Ladle
Mugs

1. Combine ingredients in kettle. Bring to boil on MEDIUM HIGH; reduce to LOW and simmer 1 hour.
2. Strain wassail; discard cinnamon and cloves.
3. Ladle equal amounts into mugs and serve hot.

Angel Food Snowstorm Cake . . . . Makes 10 servings

INGREDIENTS:

1 angel food or chiffon cake
1 carton (4 ounces)
  frozen whipped topping, thawed
2 2/3 cups (2 cans) flaked coconut

EQUIPMENT:

Measuring cups
Serving plate
Rubber spatula

1. Place cake in center of serving plate.
2. Frost cake with whipped topping using spatula.
3. Sprinkle frosted cake with coconut. Refrigerate until serving time.
4. Store leftovers in refrigerator.

Christmas Treasure Muffins . . . . Makes 18 muffins

INGREDIENTS:

1 package (14 ounces)
  banana quick bread mix
2 eggs
1 cup milk
1/4 cup vegetable oil
1 cup miniature semi-sweet
  chocolate chips
1/2 cup dried fruit bits
  Butter and jam, optional

EQUIPMENT:

Muffin papers
Measuring cups and spoons
Muffin tins
Mixing spoon
Large mixing bowl

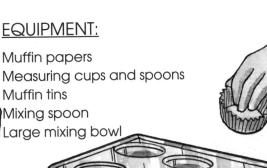

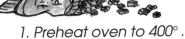

1. Preheat oven to 400°.
2. Line muffin tins with muffin papers.
3. Combine bread mix, eggs, milk, and oil in mixing bowl and beat 30 seconds with mixing spoon.
4. Add chocolate chips and fruit bits to mixture with mixing spoon.
5. Fill each muffin cup 3/4 full with mixture and bake 18 to 20 minutes or until lightly browned. Serve warm with butter and jam, if desired.

Festive Layered Cake . . . . **Makes 8 servings**

INGREDIENTS:

1   prepared cake (angel food, pound, or other)
1   carton (4 ounces) frozen whipped topping, thawed
1/2   teaspoon almond extract
1/2   cup chocolate fudge topping, room temperature, optional
  Additional chocolate fudge topping
1   package sliced almonds

EQUIPMENT:

Knife
Measuring cups and spoons
Small mixing bowl
Mixing spoon
Cake plate
Rubber spatula

1. Cut cake horizontally with knife into 3 or 4 layers and set aside.
2. Blend whipped topping and almond extract in bowl with mixing spoon until blended. Fold in fudge topping, if desired, with spatula.
3. Spread 1/4 cup of mixture onto each cake layer with spatula.
4. Center and stack layers of cake on cake plate and then frost sides with mixture using spatula.
5. Top cake with additional fudge topping and sliced almonds.
6. Cover cake and chill in refrigerator until ready to serve. Store leftovers in refrigerator.

Mrs. Claus's Chocolate Cheesecake .... Makes 9 servings

INGREDIENTS:

1/2 cup cold water
1 envelope unflavored gelatin
1/4 cup sugar
2 packages (8 ounces each)
cream cheese, softened
1/2 cup cocoa
1 1/3 cups (14 ounces)
sweetened condensed milk
Whipped topping
Red or green candied cherries
Cocoa crumb crust

EQUIPMENT:

Measuring cups and spoons
Small microwave-safe mixing bowl
Mixing spoon
Large mixing bowl
Electric mixer
Aluminum foil

1. Pour cold water into small mixing bowl
and sprinkle gelatin onto water. Let stand 5 minutes.
2. Microwave on HIGH for 1 to 1 1/2 minutes or until gelatin is dissolved. (Water
will look clear when stirred.) Carefully remove mixture from oven.
3. Add sugar to mixture and stir until dissolved; set aside.
4. Beat cream cheese and cocoa in large mixing bowl with
mixer until smooth and well-blended.
5. Add condensed milk to creamed mixture and mix with mixing spoon until smooth.
6. Add gelatin-sugar mixture to creamed mixture and beat until smooth.
7. Pour mixture into cocoa crumb crust.
8. Cover cheesecake with aluminum foil and chill in refrigerator overnight.
9. Top cake with whipped topping and candied cherries before serving.
10. Store leftovers in refrigerator.

Holiday Mints . . . . **Makes 4 to 4 1/2 dozen**

INGREDIENTS:

1/2 16-ounce package confectioners' sugar
1/4 cup margarine, softened
1 tablespoon evaporated milk
2 or 3 drops peppermint flavoring
Food coloring

EQUIPMENT:

Measuring cups and spoons
Mixing bowl
Mixing spoon
Electric mixer
Knife
Paper towels
Baking sheets

1. Combine all ingredients in mixing bowl and beat at high speed with electric mixer until well blended; then knead until smooth.
2. Shape dough into a 1/2" thick roll; cut into slices 1/2" thick.
3. Place slices on paper towel-covered baking sheets.
4. Let patties stand overnight to harden.

Cocoa Snowballs . . . . **Makes 5 dozen pieces**

INGREDIENTS:

3 1/2 cups confectioners' sugar
3/4 cup cocoa
1 1/3 cups (14-ounce can) sweetened condensed milk
1 teaspoon vanilla
2 cups chopped walnuts
Additional confectioners' sugar

EQUIPMENT:

Measuring cups and spoons
Large mixing bowl
Mixing spoon
Aluminum foil
Airtight container

1. Combine confectioners' sugar and cocoa in mixing bowl and stir with mixing spoon.
2. Add condensed milk and vanilla to mixture, blending until smooth. Stir in walnuts.
3. Cover bowl tightly with foil and chill in refrigerator for 30 minutes.
4. Shape mixture into 1" balls; then roll in confectioners' sugar.
5. Place balls in an airtight container and chill in refrigerator at least 2 hours before serving.

Santa's Dotted Swiss . . . . Makes about 4 dozen pieces

INGREDIENTS:

2 cups semi-sweet
chocolate chips
Colored candy
Sprinkles

EQUIPMENT:

Measuring cups
10" x 15" baking sheet
Wax paper
3-cup glass measure

Mixing spoon
Rubber spatula
Airtight container

1. Line baking sheet with wax paper.
2. Pour chocolate chips into measure and microwave on HIGH for 1 minute; stir with mixing spoon. Microwave on HIGH 30 seconds more; stir again.
3. Microwave chips on HIGH for another 15 to 30 seconds or until melted and hot; carefully remove chips from oven and stir with mixing spoon.
4. Spread chocolate with rubber spatula to desired thickness on lined baking sheet.
5. Shake sprinkles immediately over chocolate; let cool completely.
6. Break into pieces before serving. Store in an airtight container.

Jack Frost Fudge . . . . Makes 5 dozen pieces

INGREDIENTS:

Butter
1/4 cup milk
2 cups (12-ounce package)
milk chocolate chips
2 cups miniature marshmallows
1/2 cup chopped nuts
Dash of salt

EQUIPMENT:

8" square glass baking dish
Measuring cups and spoons
Medium saucepan
Long-handled spoon
Spatula
Knife
Airtight container

1. Grease baking dish with butter.
2. Combine milk and chocolate chips in saucepan. Cook over LOW heat until chips melt, stirring constantly with spoon.
3. Carefully remove from heat; stir in marshmallows, nuts, and salt.
4. Use spatula to spread fudge in baking dish.
5. Refrigerate until firm, then cut into 1" squares. Store in an airtight container.

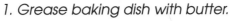

Holly Berry Haystacks . . . . Makes 3 dozen

INGREDIENTS:

Butter
1/2 cup white sugar
1/2 cup white corn syrup
1/2 cup peanut butter
2 cups Chinese noodles
1/2 cup salted peanuts

EQUIPMENT:

Wax paper
Measuring cups and spoons
Small saucepan
Spoon
Wooden spoon
Airtight container

1. Grease wax paper with butter.
2. Combine sugar and corn syrup in saucepan and stir with wooden spoon.
3. Cook over MEDIUM heat for 5 minutes or until the mixture comes to a full boil.
4. Carefully remove from heat and stir in peanut butter.
5. Add noodles and peanuts to the mixture and stir with wooden spoon until coated.
6. Drop by teaspoonfuls onto greased wax paper.
7. Let stand 15 to 20 minutes or until firm before serving. Store in an airtight container.

MED

Kris Kringle Kisses . . . . Makes 2 dozen

INGREDIENTS:

1/3 cup peanut butter
1/3 cup corn syrup
1/3 cup confectioners' sugar
1/2 cup nonfat dry milk
Chopped nuts, optional

EQUIPMENT:

Measuring cups
Small mixing bowl
Electric mixer
Sifter

Wax paper
Airtight container
Mixing spoon

1. Cream peanut butter and corn syrup in mixing bowl with mixer.
2. Sift confectioners' sugar with sifter. Gradually add sugar
and nonfat dry milk to peanut butter mixture with mixing spoon.
3. Shape dough into a roll 3/4" thick in diameter;
roll in chopped nuts, if desired.

4. Wrap roll in wax paper and chill in refrigerator for 2 hours.
5. Cut roll into twenty-four 1" pieces before serving.
Store in an airtight container.

Chocolate Pixies . . . . Makes 6 dozen

INGREDIENTS:

1 1/4 cups butter or margarine, softened
   2 cups sugar
   2 eggs
   2 teaspoons vanilla
   2 cups all-purpose flour
 3/4 cup cocoa
   1 teaspoon baking soda
   1 teaspoon salt
   2 cups well-drained maraschino cherries
   1 cup chopped nuts
   Maraschino cherries or walnut halves, optional

EQUIPMENT:

Measuring cups and spoons
Electric mixer
2 large mixing bowls
Mixing spoon
Knife
10" x 15" baking sheet
Wire rack
Airtight container

1. Preheat oven to 350°.

2. Cream butter and sugar with mixer in mixing bowl until fluffy.

3. Add eggs and vanilla to creamed mixture and beat well.

4. In the other mixing bowl, combine flour, cocoa, baking soda, and salt. Gradually add to creamed mixture with mixing spoon.

5. Finely chop cherries with knife.

6. Stir in cherries and nuts with mixing spoon.

7. Drop by teaspoonfuls onto ungreased baking sheet.

8. Garnish cookies with cherries or walnut halves, if desired.

9. Bake 10 to 12 minutes. Let cool on baking sheet 3 to 4 minutes.

10. Place cookies on rack to cool completely. Store in an airtight container.

St. Nick's Sugar Drops . . . . **Makes 2 dozen**

INGREDIENTS:

    1   package (15 ounces) sugar cookie mix
    1   cup candy-coated chocolate pieces
 1/4   cup red or green sugar crystals

EQUIPMENT:

Measuring cups and spoons
Mixing bowl
Mixing spoon
Aluminum foil
10" x 15" baking sheet
Wire rack
Airtight container

1. Prepare cookie dough in mixing bowl according to package directions.

2. Stir in candy-coated chocolate pieces with mixing spoon.

3. Cover dough with aluminum foil and chill in refrigerator 30 minutes.

4. Preheat oven to 375°.

5. Shape dough into 1 1/2" balls.

6. Roll balls in sugar crystals.

7. Place balls 2 inches apart on ungreased baking sheet.

8. Bake 10 to 12 minutes. Let cool on baking sheet 3 to 4 minutes.

9. Place cookies on rack to cool completely. Store in an airtight container.

Christmas Cookie Trees . . . . Makes 6 trees

INGREDIENTS:

4 cups toasted oat cereal
32 large marshmallows
   or 3 cups miniature marshmallows
3 tablespoons butter
   or margarine
1/2 teaspoon vanilla
1/2 teaspoon green food coloring
   Additional butter
   Small gumdrops

EQUIPMENT:

Measuring cups and spoons
Large mixing bowl
Medium-size saucepan
Mixing spoon
10" x 15" baking sheet
Scissors
Plastic wrap

1. Empty cereal into mixing bowl.
2. Combine marshmallows and butter in saucepan; cook over MEDIUM heat until marshmallows melt, stirring constantly with mixing spoon until smooth.
3. Carefully remove from heat. Stir in vanilla and food coloring with mixing spoon.
4. Pour marshmallow mixture over cereal and stir with mixing spoon until the cereal is coated.
5. Grease baking sheet with butter.
6. Coat hands with butter and divide the cereal mixture into 6 parts on the baking sheet, using about 2/3 cup for each.
7. Shape each part into a Christmas tree.
8. Cut gumdrops into slices with scissors. (Dip the scissors into a glass of water to prevent candy from sticking.)
9. Press gumdrop slices onto the trees.
10. Wrap trees in plastic wrap to store.

Elf Print Cookies. . . . . Makes 5 dozen

INGREDIENTS:

    1   cup butter or margarine, softened
1 3/4   cups packed light brown sugar
    2   eggs
    2   teaspoons vanilla
    3   cups all-purpose flour
    1   teaspoon baking powder
    1   teaspoon salt
    2   cups (12-ounce package)
        peanut butter chips
1 1/2   cups quick-cooking rolled oats
  3/4   cup jelly or preserves
        (apple, grape, or peach)

EQUIPMENT:

Measuring cups and spoons
2 large mixing bowls
Electric mixer
Mixing spoon
10" x 15" baking sheet
Wire rack
Airtight container

1. Preheat oven to 400°.
2. Cream butter and brown sugar in mixing bowl with mixer
   until fluffy; add vanilla and eggs to mixture and beat well.
3. In the other mixing bowl, combine flour, baking powder, and salt.
   Gradually add to creamed mixture with mixing spoon.
4. Set aside 1/2 cup peanut butter chips.
5. Stir in remaining peanut butter chips and oats with mixing spoon.
6. Shape dough into 1" balls and place on ungreased baking sheet.
7. Press center of each ball with thumb to make indention about 1" wide.
8. Bake 7 to 9 minutes. Let cool on baking sheet 3 to 4 minutes.
9. Place cookies on rack to cool completely.
10. Fill the center of each cookie with 1/2 teaspoon jelly;
    Store in an airtight container.

Santa's Surprise Cookies . . . . Makes 4 dozen

INGREDIENTS:

  1 cup butter, softened
1/2 cup sugar
  1 teaspoon vanilla
  2 cups all-purpose flour
  1 cup ground walnuts
  1 package (9 ounces)
     chocolate drops, unwrapped
     Additional butter
     Confectioners' sugar, optional

EQUIPMENT:

Measuring cups and spoons
Electric mixer
Large mixing bowl
Electric blender
Mixing spoon
10" x 15" baking sheet
Wire rack
Airtight container

1. Preheat oven to 350°.
2. Cream butter and sugar with mixer in mixing bowl until fluffy.
3. Pour walnuts into blender container and cover.
4. Blend on HIGH until walnuts are ground.
5. Add walnuts, vanilla, and flour to mixture and blend with mixing spoon.
6. Roll small amount of dough into a ball around each chocolate drop
so that drop is completely covered.
7. Grease baking sheet with butter.
8. Place balls on cookie sheet and bake 10 minutes.
9. While still warm, roll balls in confectioners' sugar, if desired.
10. Cool cookies on wire rack.
11. Store cookies in an airtight container.

Fruit-Jeweled Drops................Makes 3 dozen

INGREDIENTS:

1/3 cup butter or margarine, softened
2 tablespoons sugar
1 egg
1 package (8 ounces) white
    or yellow cake mix
1/2 cup red candied cherries
1/2 cup green candied cherries
1/2 cup candied pineapple chunks
1 cup (6-ounce package)
    semi-sweet chocolate chips

EQUIPMENT:

Measuring cups and spoons
Large mixing bowl
Electric mixer
Mixing spoon
Knife
10" x 15" baking sheet
Wire rack

1. Preheat oven to 375°.
2. Cream butter and sugar in mixing bowl with mixer until fluffy.
3. Add egg to creamed mixture and beat well.
4. Gradually add cake mix to creamed mixture with mixing
   spoon, blending until smooth.
5. Chop cherries and pineapple into small pieces with knife.
6. Stir in cherries, pineapple, and chocolate chips with mixing spoon.
7. Drop by teaspoons onto ungreased baking sheet.
8. Bake 10 to 12 minutes. Let cool on baking sheet 3 to 4 minutes.
9. Place cookies on rack to cool completely.
   Store in an airtight container.

Peppermint Delights . . . . Makes 3 dozen

INGREDIENTS:

1 cup butter or margarine, softened
1 cup confectioners' sugar
2 teaspoons vanilla
1 1/2 cups all-purpose flour
1/2 teaspoon salt
1/4 cup peppermint candy
1 cup quick-cooking rolled oats
Red or green food coloring, optional
Additional confectioners' sugar

EQUIPMENT:

Measuring cups and spoons
Large mixing bowl
Electric mixer
Sifter
Mixing spoon
Rolling pin
Cookie cutters
Wire rack
10" x 15" baking sheet
Airtight container

1. Preheat oven to 325°.
2. Cream butter and 1 cup sugar in mixing bowl with mixer until fluffy.
3. Add vanilla to creamed mixture and beat well.
4. Sift flour and salt together with sifter; gradually add to creamed mixture with mixing spoon.
5. Tint dough with red or green food coloring, if desired.
6. Crush peppermint candy with rolling pin.
7. Fold in candy and rolled oats with mixing spoon, mixing just until dough holds together.
8. Sift confectioners' sugar onto countertop with sifter.
9. Roll out dough 1/8" thick on a countertop sprinkled with confectioners' sugar.
10. Cut out cookies with cookie cutters, sprinkle lightly with confectioners' sugar, and place on ungreased baking sheet.
11. Bake 15 minutes. Let cool on baking sheet 3 to 4 minutes.
12. Place cookies on rack to cool completely. Store in airtight container.

SNACKS

Reindeer Nibble . . . . Makes about 5 1/2 cups

INGREDIENTS:

- 1 cup dried apples
- 1 cup dried apricots
- 1 cup flaked coconut
- 1 cup raisins
- 1 cup carob chips, optional
- 1/2 pound cashews
- 1/2 pound pecans
- 1/2 pound almonds

EQUIPMENT:

- Knife
- Measuring cup
- Large mixing bowl
- Mixing spoon
- Airtight container

1. Chop dried apples and apricots in half with knife.
2. Combine all ingredients in mixing bowl with mixing spoon.
3. Store in an airtight container.

Christmas Party Crunch. . . . . Makes 4 servings

INGREDIENTS:

- 1/2 cup butter or margarine
- 1 tablespoon soy sauce
- 1/4 teaspoon garlic salt
- 1/4 teaspoon onion salt
- 1 can (5 ounces) Chinese noodles or 1 cup pretzel sticks
- 1 cup square rice cereal
- 1 cup peanuts

EQUIPMENT:

- Measuring cups and spoons
- Microwave-safe mixing bowl
- Wooden mixing spoon
- 10" x 15" jelly roll pan
- Airtight container

1. Preheat oven to 275°.
2. Microwave butter in mixing bowl on MEDIUM for 30 seconds or until melted. Carefully remove bowl from microwave oven.
3. Add soy sauce and garlic and onion salts; stir with wooden mixing spoon.
4. Spread Chinese noodles, rice cereal, and peanuts on jelly roll pan.
5. Drizzle with butter mixture and stir with wooden spoon to coat.
6. Bake 5 minutes; stir well and bake another 5 minutes or until light brown.
7. Remove from oven.
8. Let cool completely. Store in an airtight container.

Sleighbell Squares...................Makes 2 dozen

INGREDIENTS:

2 cups corn flakes
2/3 cup packed light brown sugar
1 cup light corn syrup
2 cups (12-ounce package) peanut butter chips
2 tablespoons vegetable oil
2 teaspoons vanilla
4 cups crisp rice cereal
Butter

EQUIPMENT:

Measuring cups and spoons
2 large mixing bowls
9" x 13" glass baking dish
Large saucepan
Wooden spoon
Rubber spatula
Airtight container
Knife

1. Pour corn flakes into mixing bowl and lightly crush with hands.

2. Grease baking dish with butter.

3. Combine corn syrup and brown sugar in a large saucepan
and bring to a full boil over MEDIUM heat. Stir constantly with wooden spoon.

4. Add peanut butter chips and oil to mixture and stir with wooden spoon until chips are melted.

5. Carefully remove from heat and stir in vanilla with wooden spoon.

6. Add rice cereal and corn flakes to mixture and stir thoroughly with wooden spoon to coat.

7. Press mixture into baking dish with spatula.

8. Let cool completely; then cut into squares with knife. Store in an airtight container.

25

Jolly S'Mores................................Makes 1 serving

INGREDIENTS:

2 graham cracker squares
1 tablespoon peanut butter
1 tablespoon marshmallow creme
1/2 chocolate bar

EQUIPMENT:

Measuring spoon
Knife

1. Spread peanut butter with knife on 1 graham cracker square.
2. Top peanut butter with chocolate bar.
3. Spread marshmallow creme on remaining graham cracker square.
4. Place marshmallow-side down on the chocolate bar.

Merry Mexican Munch ....Makes 8 cups

INGREDIENTS:

1/2 cup butter
1 tablespoon taco seasoning mix
2 cups corn chips
2 cups crisp corn cereal squares
1 cup crisp rice cereal squares
1 cup peanuts
2 cups pretzel sticks

EQUIPMENT:

Measuring cups and spoons
1-cup glass measure
Fork
9" x 13" glass baking dish
Airtight container

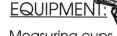

1. Place butter in glass measure and microwave on HIGH for 1 minute or until butter is melted.
2. Carefully remove from oven and add taco seasoning mix. Stir with fork; set aside.
3. Combine chips, cereals, pretzels, and peanuts in baking dish with mixing spoon.
4. Drizzle with butter mixture and stir with fork.
5. Microwave mixture on HIGH for 2 minutes; then stir with fork.
6. Microwave mixture on HIGH another 1 to 2 minutes until thoroughly heated.
7. Carefully remove mixture from oven. Cool completely before serving.
Store mixture in an airtight container.

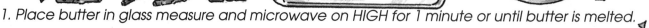

Mistletoe Treats . . . . **Makes 2 dozen**

INGREDIENTS:

Butter
1 package (14 ounces) caramels
3 tablespoons water
1 cup crisp corn cereal squares
1 cup bran cereal squares
1 cup crispy rice cereal
1 cup granola
1/2 cup shredded coconut
1 1/2 cups salted peanuts
1/2 cup milk chocolate chips
1 tablespoon shortening

EQUIPMENT:

9" x 13" glass baking dish
Microwave-safe mixing bowl
Measuring cups and spoons
Wooden spoon
Large mixing bowl
Mixing spoon
1-cup glass measure
Knife
Airtight container

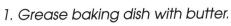

1. Grease baking dish with butter.
2. Remove wrappers from caramels. Place caramels
in microwave-safe mixing bowl and add water.
3. Microwave caramels on HIGH for 1 minute. Stir caramels with wooden spoon.
4. Microwave caramels on HIGH for another 1 1/2 to 2 minutes or until melted and hot.
Carefully remove bowl from oven and stir with wooden spoon.
5. Combine cereals, granola, coconut, and peanuts in
large mixing bowl and stir with mixing spoon.
6. Carefully drizzle caramel over cereal mixture; then stir with wooden spoon to coat.
7. Pour mixture into buttered baking dish.
8. Grease back of spoon with butter and gently press mixture evenly into the dish.
9. Pour chocolate chips into glass measure and microwave on HIGH for 1 minute.
Stir chips with mixing spoon. Add shortening to mixture.
10. Microwave on HIGH for another 1 to 1 1/2 minutes or until melted and hot;
carefully remove from oven and stir with mixing spoon.
11. Slowly drizzle chocolate over mixture in thin lines across the top.
12. Chill mixture 30 minutes or until chocolate is completely cooled.
13. Cut mixture into squares with knife before serving. Store in an airtight container.

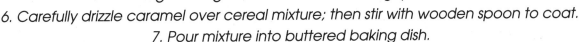

Santa's Super Smackers ....**Makes 2 Super Smackers**

INGREDIENTS:

20 Large marshmallows
3 tablespoons butter
1/2 cup semi-sweet
    chocolate chips
3 cups crisp rice cereal
Additional butter

EQUIPMENT:

Measuring cups and spoons
Large microwave-safe mixing bowl
Wooden spoon
2 12" x 12" squares wax paper
2 12" x 12" squares aluminum foil

1. Combine marshmallows, butter, and chocolate chips in mixing bowl.
2. Microwave mixture on high for 1 minute. Marshmallows will puff up; stir down with wooden spoon.
3. Microwave on HIGH for another 20 to 30 seconds until marshmallows and chocolate chips are melted.
4. Carefully remove mixture from oven and stir in cereal with wooden spoon to coat.
5. Pour 1/2 of the mixture onto one square of wax paper.
6. Grease hands with butter; then shape mixture into a large cone-shape, rounded at the base and pointed at the top. Repeat with remaining mixture.
7. Let the cones dry for 20 to 30 minutes or until they are no longer sticky.
8. Wrap each cone in foil, twisting foil at top to resemble a candy kiss.

Prancer's Peanut Butter . . . . **Makes 1 cup**

INGREDIENTS

2 1/2 cups salted peanuts
2 tablespoons butter
    or margarine, softened

EQUIPMENT:

Measuring cups and spoons
Electric blender
Rubber spatula
Small jar with lid

1. Set aside 1/2 cup peanuts.
2. Pour remaining peanuts into blender container.
3. Cover and blend peanuts on LOW until the peanuts are chopped.
4. Add butter to chopped peanuts. Cover and blend mixture on LOW for 10 seconds.
5. Turn off blender; then scrape sides with spatula.
6. Cover and blend mixture on LOW for 5 seconds. Repeat until mixture is smooth.
7. Cover and blend mixture on HIGH for 1 minute.
8. Add remaining peanuts to mixture; then cover and blend for 3 seconds.
9. Empty the peanut butter into jar and screw on lid.
10. Chill peanut butter in refrigerator for 30 minutes before serving.
11. Keep refrigerated.

Blitzen's Brittle . . . . **Makes 3 dozen pieces**

INGREDIENTS:

1 cup sugar
1/2 cup white corn syrup
1 cup peanuts
1/8 teaspoon salt
1 teaspoon butter
1 teaspoon vanilla
1 teaspoon baking soda

EQUIPMENT:

Large microwave-safe mixing bowl
Measuring spoons
Mixing spoon
Cookie sheet

1. Mix together sugar, corn syrup, peanuts, and salt.
2. Microwave on HIGH for 4 minutes.
3. Stir and microwave for 3 to 5 minutes more, until the syrup is light brown.
4. Add butter and vanilla and blend well.
5. Microwave 1 to 2 minutes more until peanuts are browned.
6. Add baking soda and stir well. The mixture will foam up.
7. Pour onto greased cookie sheet and cool.
8. Break into pieces. Store in airtight container.

Christmas Nut Rolls..................Makes 4 rolls

INGREDIENTS:

- 1 jar (7 1/2 ounces) marshmallow creme
- 1 teaspoon vanilla
- 2 1/2 cups confectioners' sugar
- 1 pound caramels, unwrapped
- 2 to 3 tablespoons water
- 6 cups chopped nuts

EQUIPMENT:

Measuring cups and spoons
Large mixing bowl
Mixing spoon
Plastic wrap
Large glass measure
Fork
Airtight container

1. Combine marshmallow creme and vanilla in mixing bowl and stir with mixing spoon; gradually stir in sugar.

2. Knead until well blended and shape mixture into 4 rolls about 1" thick in diameter; wrap in plastic and freeze 6 hours.

3. Place caramels and water in glass measure; microwave on HIGH 45 seconds.

4. Stir with mixing spoon; microwave on HIGH for 45 seconds or until melted. Carefully remove from oven.

5. Use a fork to dip rolls in caramel one side at a time. Roll in nuts until well coated.

6. Let cool completely. Store in an airtight container.

7. Slice before serving.

Jingle Bell Balls . . . . Makes 18 balls

INGREDIENTS:

Butter
4   quarts popped corn
1   cup peanuts
1   cup raisins or other dried fruit
1   cup sugar
3/4 cup light corn syrup
1   can (14 ounces)
    sweetened condensed milk
1/8 teaspoon salt
1/4 cup butter or margarine
1   teaspoon vanilla

EQUIPMENT:

Large mixing bowl
Measuring cups and spoons
Wooden spoon
Large heavy saucepan
Candy thermometer
Wax paper
Plastic wrap

MED

1. Grease mixing bowl with butter.
2. Combine popcorn, peanuts, and raisins in buttered bowl;
   stir with wooden spoon and set aside.
3. Combine sugar, corn syrup, condensed milk,
   and salt in saucepan; mix with wooden spoon.
4. Cook mixture over MEDIUM
   heat for 30 minutes or until candy
   thermometer reads 230°, stirring
   constantly with wooden spoon.
5. Carefully remove mixture from heat and allow to cool slightly.
6. Stir 1/4 cup butter and vanilla into mixture.
7. Drizzle over popcorn mixture; toss until evenly coated.
8. Let mixture cool until it is warm to the touch.
9. Grease hands and wax paper with butter.
10. Shape mixture into firm 3" balls.
11. Let balls harden on buttered wax paper. Let balls cool completely.
12. Wrap each ball with plastic wrap.

INDEX